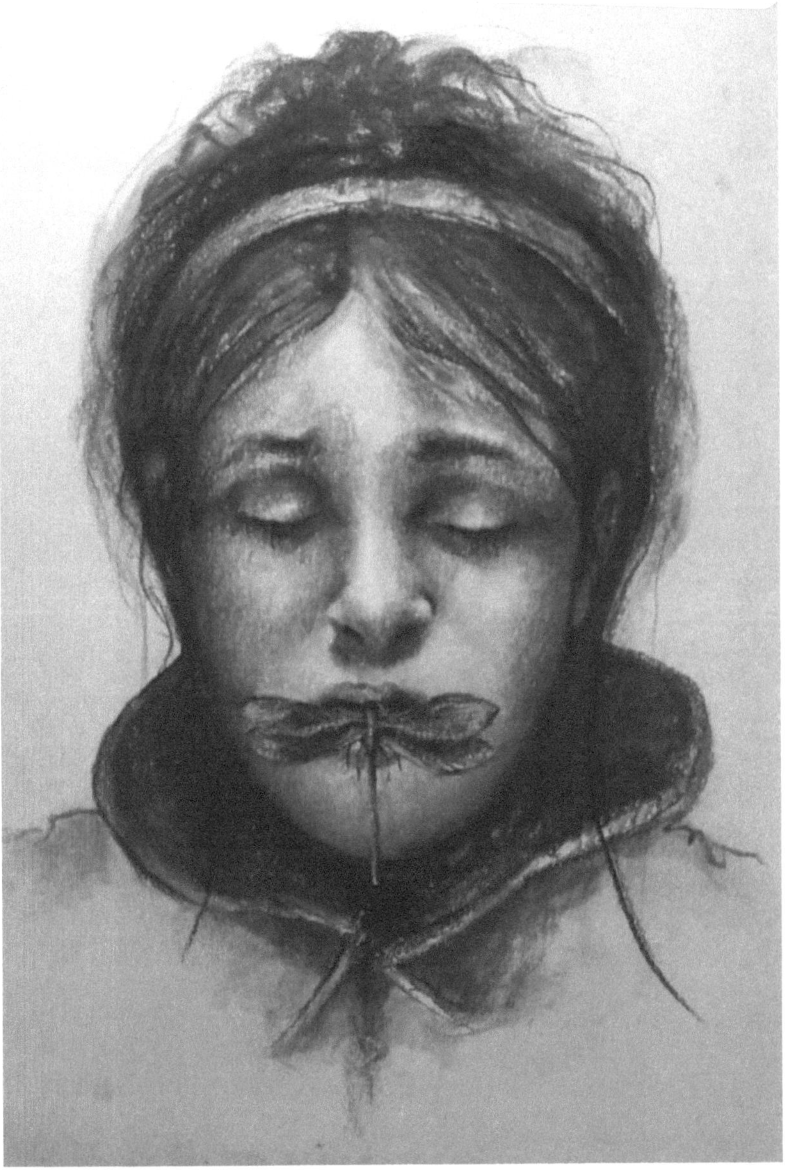

DRAGONFLY

And Other Songs of Mourning

By Michelle Scalise

LVP
PUBLICATIONS

Cover art by CANIGLIA www.jeremycaniglia.com
Cover design by Kealan Patrick Burke
Interior illustration by Luke Spooner

Dragonfly Copyright © 2019 Michelle Scalise

"Lot's Wife" first appeared in the HWA Poetry Showcase Volume 2 (2014)
"Basement" first appeared in Dark Voices (2018)

All rights reserved. No part of this book may be reproduced in any form, including in print, electronic form or by mechanical means, without written permission from the publisher, author or individual copyright holder except for in the case of a book reviewer, who may quote brief passages embedded in and as part of an article or review.

Lycan Valley Press Publications
1625 E 72nd St STE 700 PMB 132
Tacoma, Washington 98404
United States of America

Printed in the United States of America

First Edition, April 2019

ISBN-13: 978-1-64562-998-6

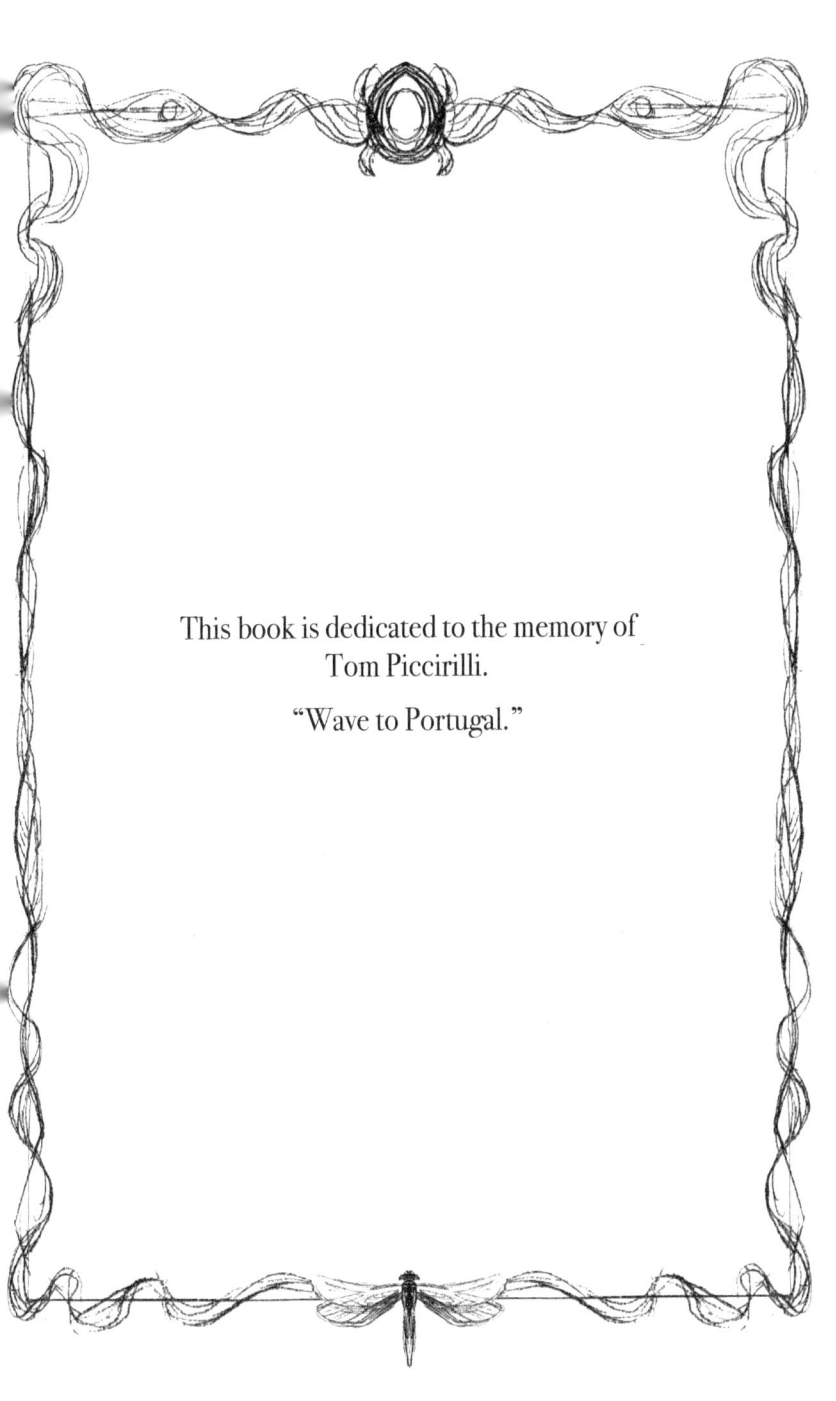

This book is dedicated to the memory of Tom Piccirilli.

"Wave to Portugal."

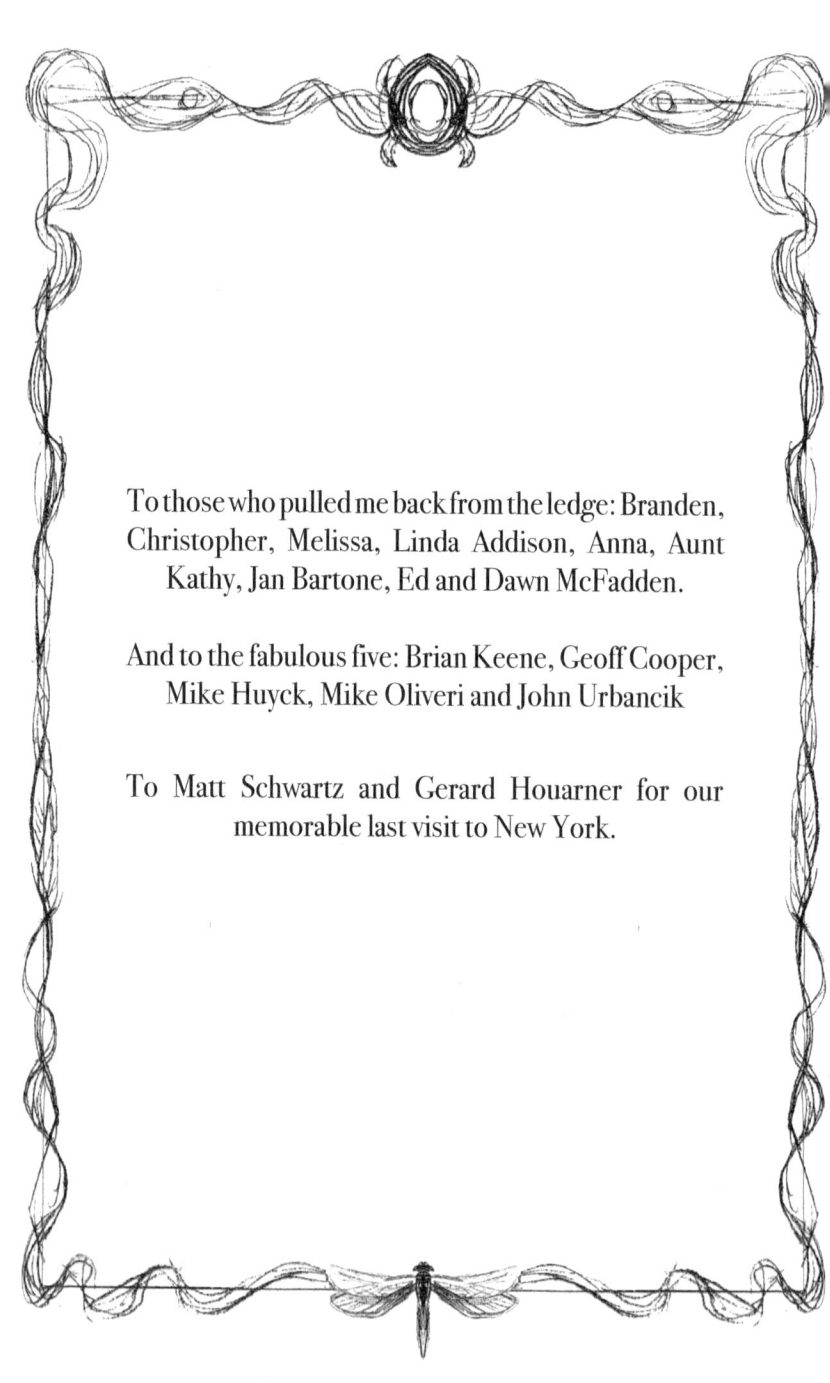

To those who pulled me back from the ledge: Branden, Christopher, Melissa, Linda Addison, Anna, Aunt Kathy, Jan Bartone, Ed and Dawn McFadden.

And to the fabulous five: Brian Keene, Geoff Cooper, Mike Huyck, Mike Oliveri and John Urbancik

To Matt Schwartz and Gerard Houarner for our memorable last visit to New York.

"Thunder means something different to everyone but rain is always the same." —Tom Piccirilli

GOVERNMENT RULES FOR WAR WIDOWS

You've several months for mourning attire
'Till they grow bored and exasperated
At the sight of you
Toughen up!
We all know someone in the war.
Loss should be worn with modesty.
We bury fallen soldiers every day.
But tell me dear,
What kind of funeral rites were those?
In lieu of flowers read a novel?
Where's your gray ribbon,
Where's your pride?
Stop exposing open wounds.
We'll accept the quiet humility
Of a disconsolate widow instead.

WORDS HE REMEMBERED

He couldn't see her anymore
Morphine shuttered his eyes
And cobwebs hung from his lashes
But he heard her whispering
And her prayers became a chapter
On the white walls of his cell.
Words dripping from the ceiling
To languish on the cracked linoleum floor.

His writing was his hunger.
Words black as the poison inside him
Spun into strings of sentences.
Both the horror and the beauty
He longed to type.

Ideas drowning in an IV bag.
Page after page
Streaming from his brain
Too quickly to catch.
He cried watching them fly away.

But he didn't grieve his own loss,
She'd do that for him.
It was the stories
He'd forgotten to tell
That ran like deer in the mountains
Through the silence he'd leave behind.

THE HALL

Doctors pat my hand,
Speak slowly
As if comforting a child
And I hate them for it.

They call her away from my bed
Into the dark
Into the hall
Time never moves as I wait.

She returns with eyes red as raspberries
Black eyeliner haphazardly
Wiped away.
She talks too quickly about nothing,
But I see the cracks.
Her lips frozen blue from the snow.
She could never lie worth a damn.

What happens to her out there?
I look to see if they've broken her fingers
But my vision is blurry from the drugs
And her hands shake so.

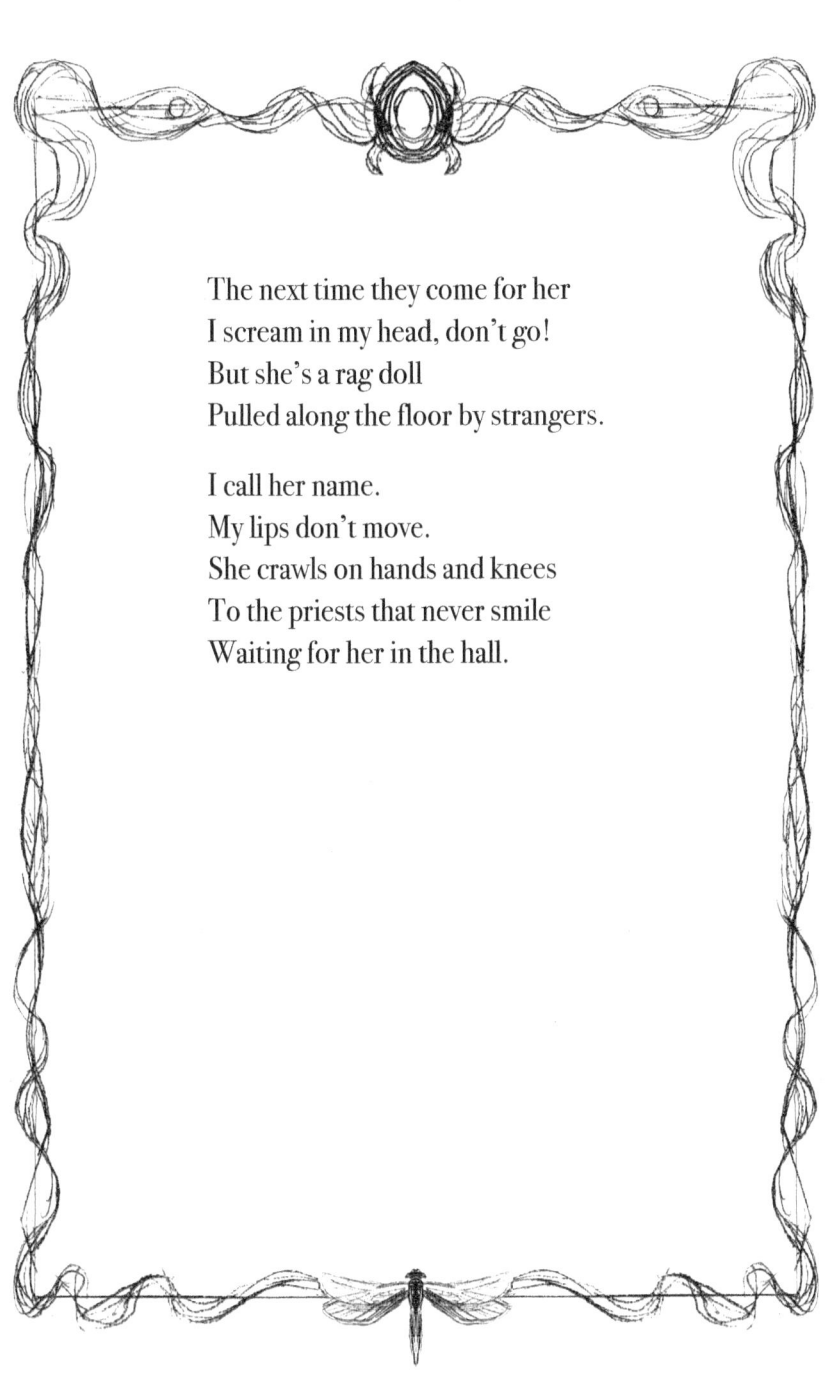

The next time they come for her
I scream in my head, don't go!
But she's a rag doll
Pulled along the floor by strangers.

I call her name.
My lips don't move.
She crawls on hands and knees
To the priests that never smile
Waiting for her in the hall.

DRAGONFLY

You remain
the shadow of a dragonfly
fluttering in dusty curtains.
Two years, my voice grows hoarse
calling you back from a void.
Can you hear me anymore?
Or have my cries become a metronome
quietly ticking away the moments
of a mad woman.

Cast adrift with pain and ashes,
everyone shrieking, "Let him go"
until the boat tossed
I lost my grip
and you were swallowed by the sea.
A black box sinking into nowhere.

There is a memory,
the silence when you stopped breathing
keeps me down and keeps me screaming.
I clench my fists until I bleed.

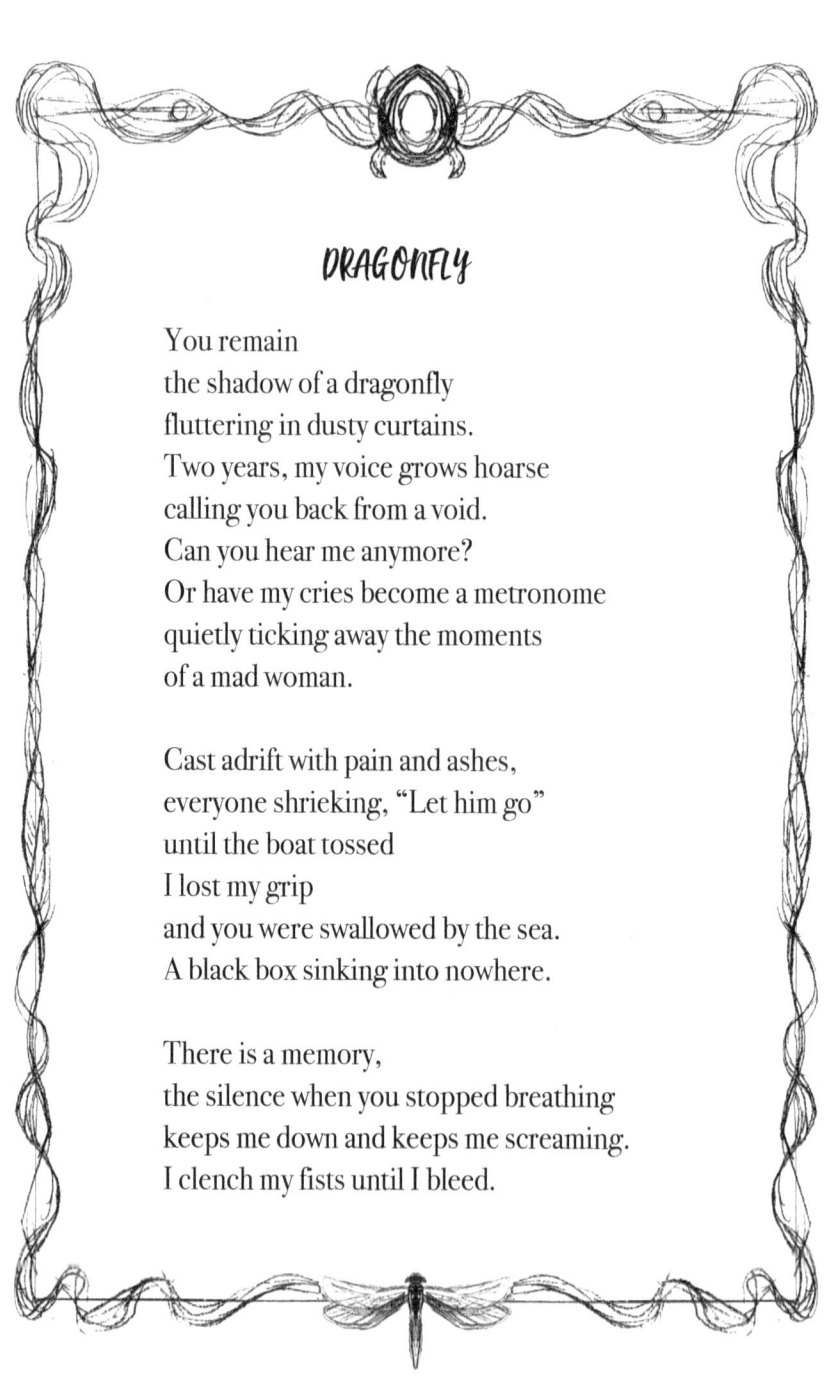

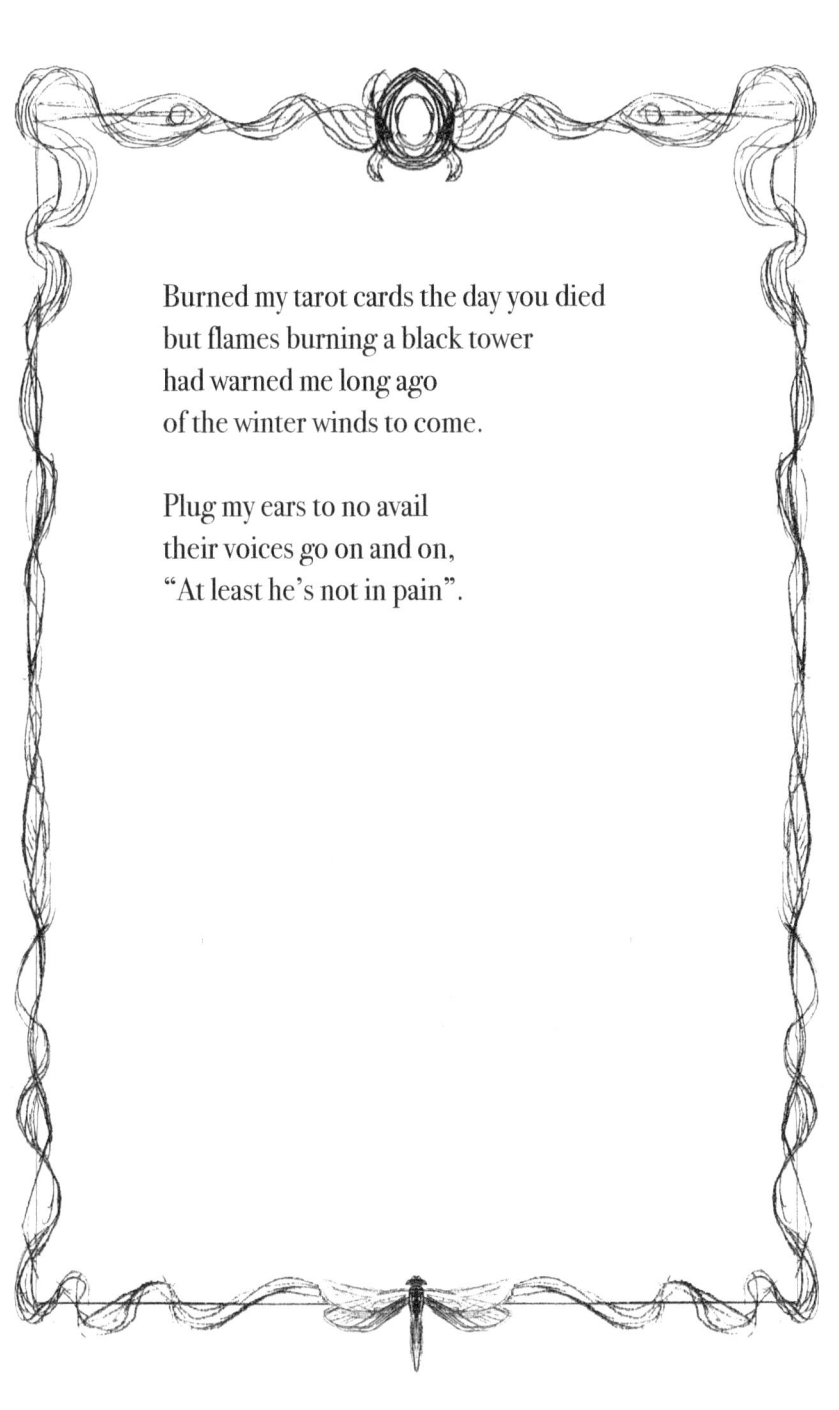

Burned my tarot cards the day you died
but flames burning a black tower
had warned me long ago
of the winter winds to come.

Plug my ears to no avail
their voices go on and on,
"At least he's not in pain".

FAILURE IS A VILE NURSE

I hang in the closet next to my wedding dress
going mad attempting to tie a noose.
Black diamonds 'round my neck,
the last kiss from a dying man
I vowed to save and failed.

Never marry a girl raised with the imprint of a junkie.
I guess college never taught you that.

At night I lie naked in the storm.
Eternity is a cold November,
the shadow of mountains all around me.
I've forgotten the warmth of the sun.

I am a poet and a failure
paralyzed in our past
with pages always open
here and here to the
paragraphs of a nightmare.

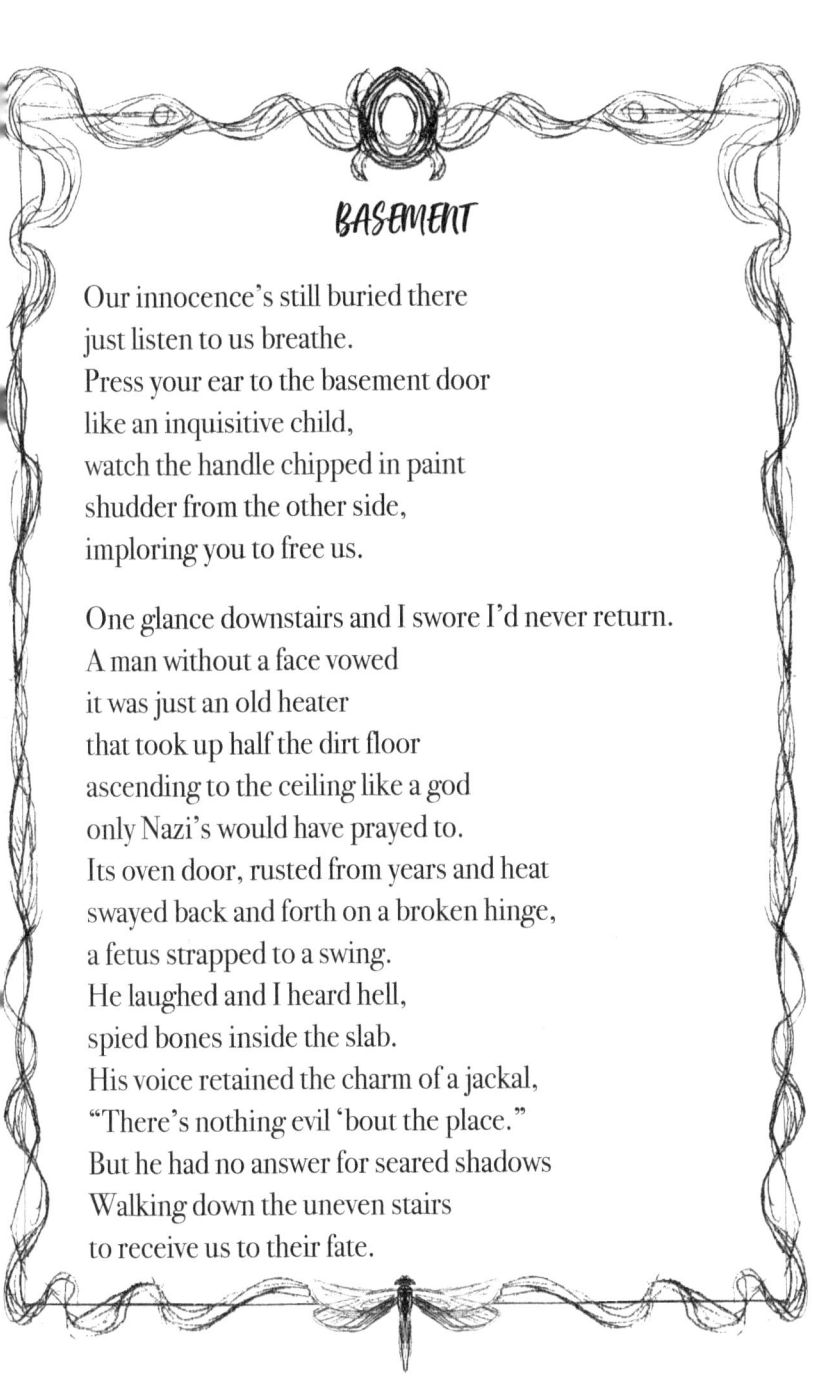

BASEMENT

Our innocence's still buried there
just listen to us breathe.
Press your ear to the basement door
like an inquisitive child,
watch the handle chipped in paint
shudder from the other side,
imploring you to free us.

One glance downstairs and I swore I'd never return.
A man without a face vowed
it was just an old heater
that took up half the dirt floor
ascending to the ceiling like a god
only Nazi's would have prayed to.
Its oven door, rusted from years and heat
swayed back and forth on a broken hinge,
a fetus strapped to a swing.
He laughed and I heard hell,
spied bones inside the slab.
His voice retained the charm of a jackal,
"There's nothing evil 'bout the place."
But he had no answer for seared shadows
Walking down the uneven stairs
to receive us to their fate.

ROOM 527

Are all the graveyard nurses sleeping,
or laying odds on who'll die at dawn?
Three doors down a woman's wailing
like a rabid animal well aware
of how she'll meet her end.

I try drowning her out and watch you sleep,
terrified her awful echoes
will seep between my desperate grasp
awakening you from the morphine,
to certainties I'll never tell.
Shut up! I scream inside,
and let him die in silence.

Into the hallway I wander like a lost soul.
Her room is clean and the bed is made.
On hands and knees howling
to dead stars, her hair
long and black scrapes the tiled floor.
I don't want to see anymore
but she turns to me and stares.
There is a buzzing in my head.
She is my anguish and my sorrow.
How could I have thought
she was anyone but me?

I AM VENGFUL DESTRUCTION

My hair drips with his blood
I smooth the folds of my wedding dress
Soiled red from times I tried to die
And an audience of three
Cheered like Victorians at a hanging.

Standing barefoot on rotting floorboards
I wonder, what's the use of quartering a woman
Half dead in the arms of pain?

The light of my misery creates stars in their eyes,
Three witches waiting for sainthood
Outside the steps of an empty church.
Guilty hands hidden in bibles
Pray like nuns when they've an audience,
So sure a crucifixion is filled with compassion
And heaven is waiting like an open bank.

One was born of a stranger's womb,
But a word of sympathy from the sandman
And she swam in accolades for a month,
The dead just an afterthought.

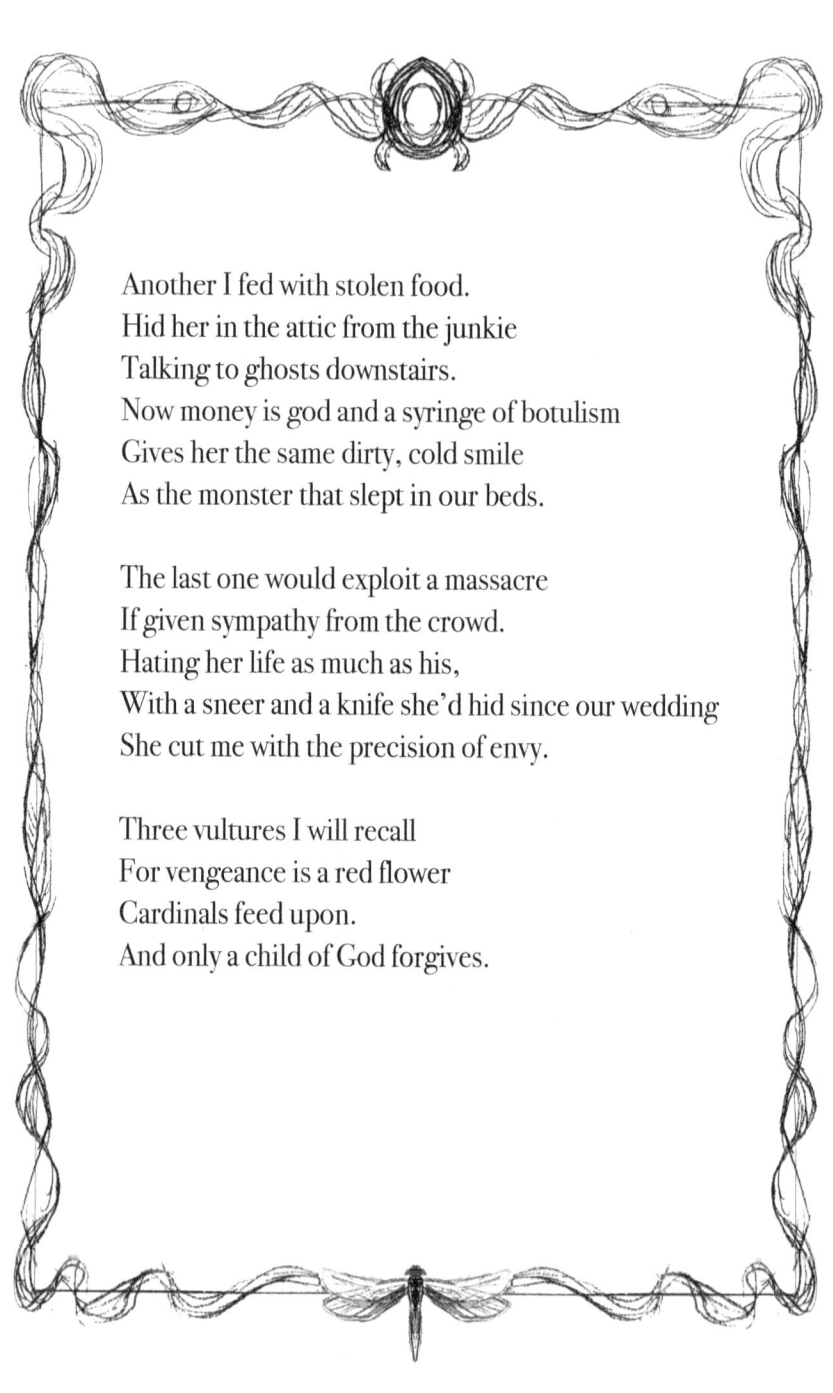

Another I fed with stolen food.
Hid her in the attic from the junkie
Talking to ghosts downstairs.
Now money is god and a syringe of botulism
Gives her the same dirty, cold smile
As the monster that slept in our beds.

The last one would exploit a massacre
If given sympathy from the crowd.
Hating her life as much as his,
With a sneer and a knife she'd hid since our wedding
She cut me with the precision of envy.

Three vultures I will recall
For vengeance is a red flower
Cardinals feed upon.
And only a child of God forgives.

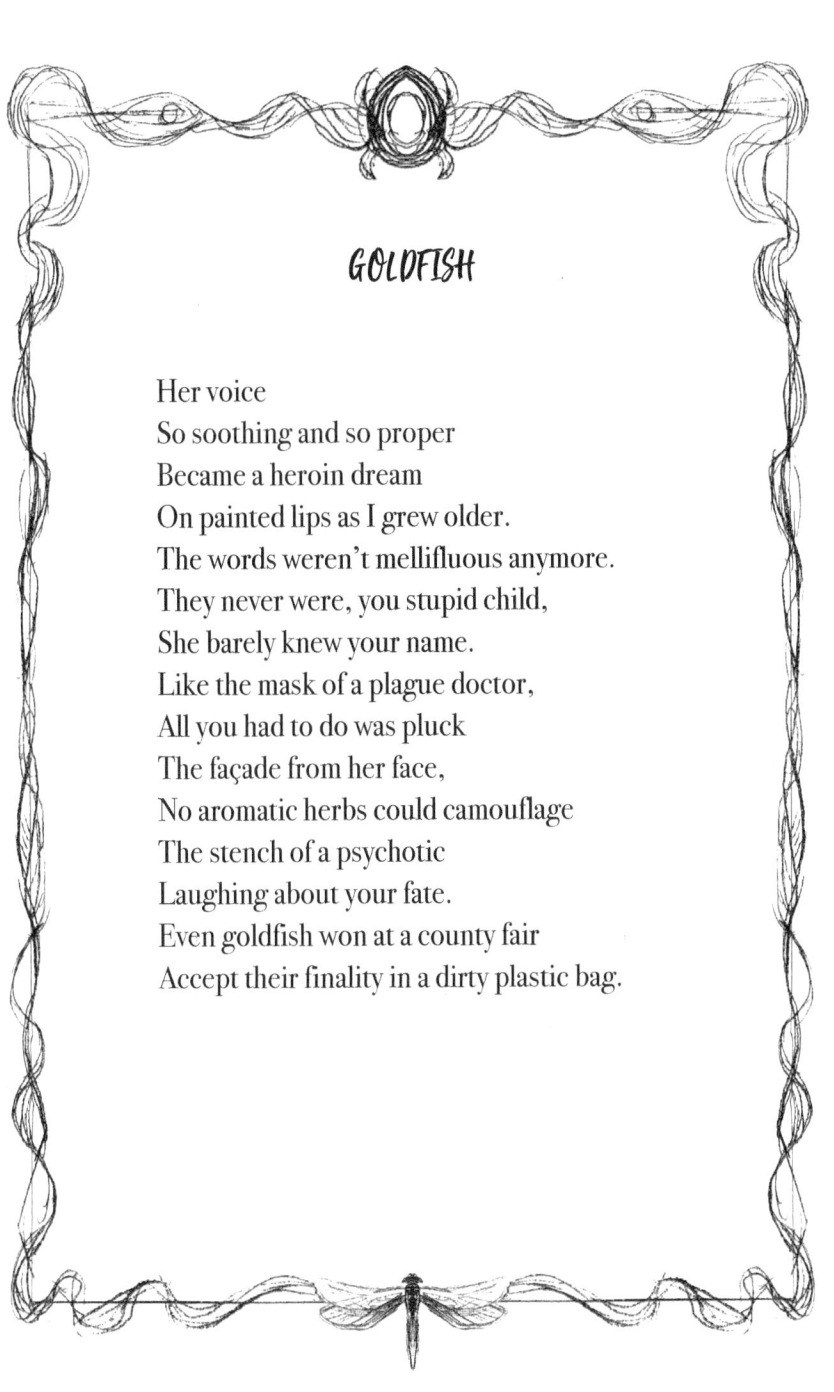

GOLDFISH

Her voice
So soothing and so proper
Became a heroin dream
On painted lips as I grew older.
The words weren't mellifluous anymore.
They never were, you stupid child,
She barely knew your name.
Like the mask of a plague doctor,
All you had to do was pluck
The façade from her face,
No aromatic herbs could camouflage
The stench of a psychotic
Laughing about your fate.
Even goldfish won at a county fair
Accept their finality in a dirty plastic bag.

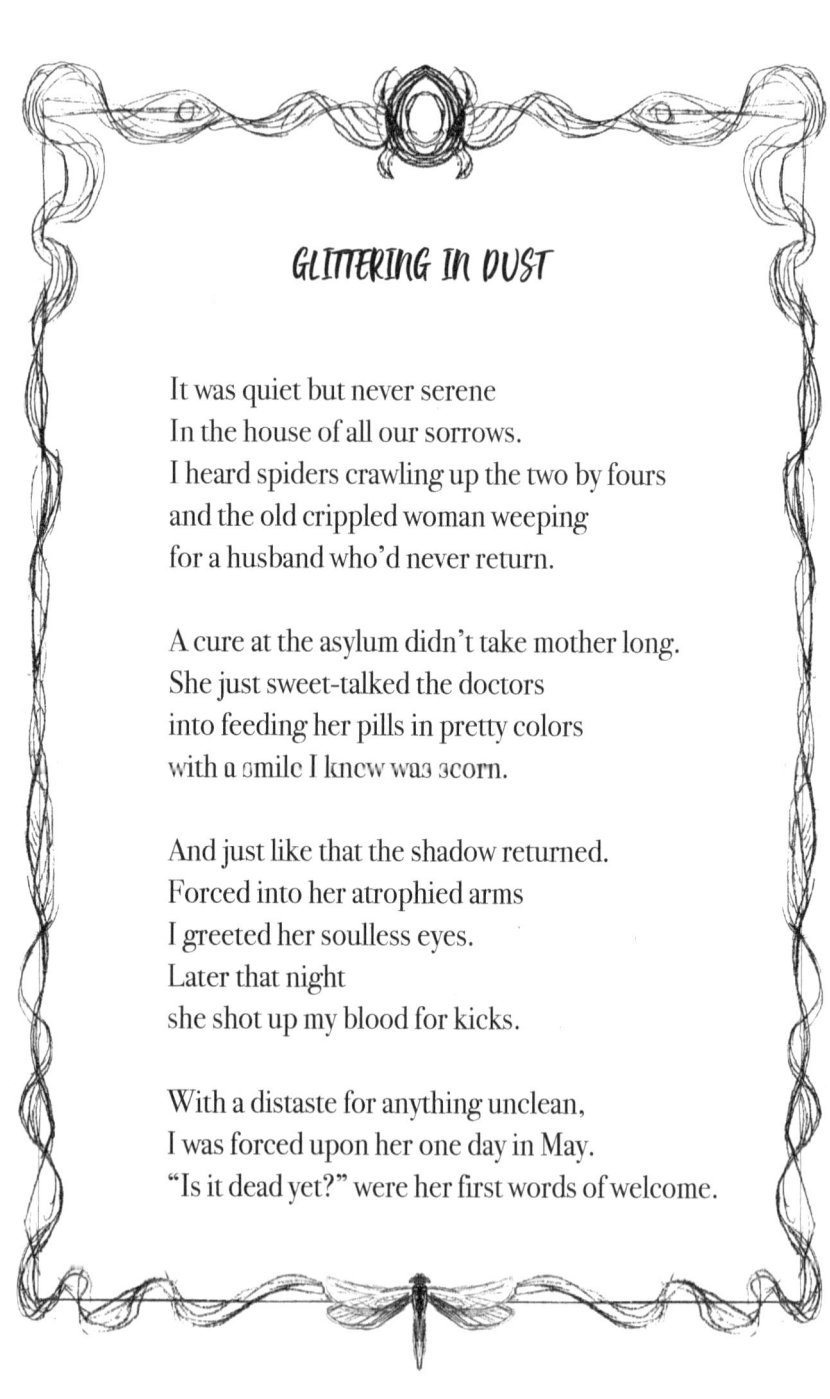

GLITTERING IN DUST

It was quiet but never serene
In the house of all our sorrows.
I heard spiders crawling up the two by fours
and the old crippled woman weeping
for a husband who'd never return.

A cure at the asylum didn't take mother long.
She just sweet-talked the doctors
into feeding her pills in pretty colors
with a smile I knew was scorn.

And just like that the shadow returned.
Forced into her atrophied arms
I greeted her soulless eyes.
Later that night
she shot up my blood for kicks.

With a distaste for anything unclean,
I was forced upon her one day in May.
"Is it dead yet?" were her first words of welcome.

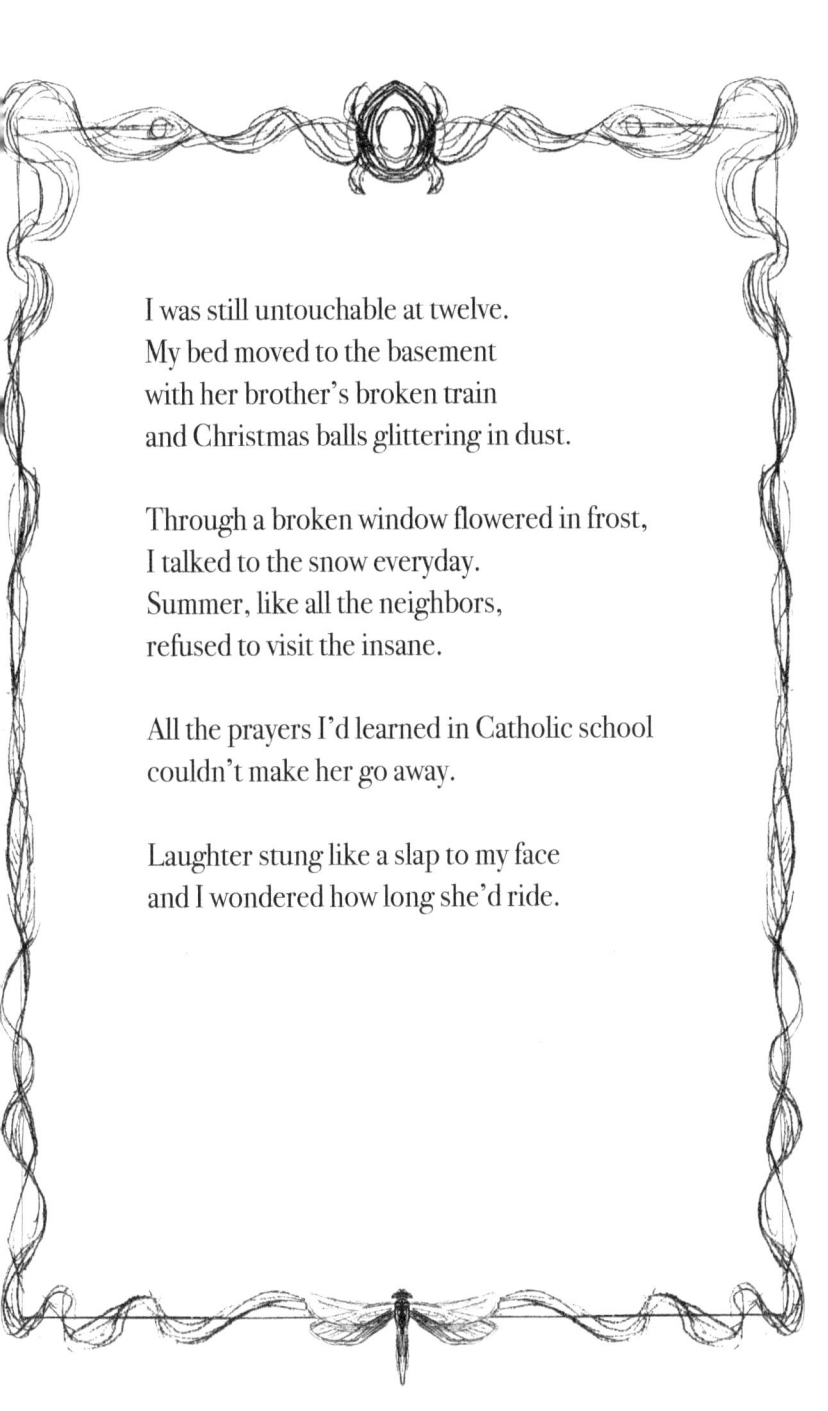

I was still untouchable at twelve.
My bed moved to the basement
with her brother's broken train
and Christmas balls glittering in dust.

Through a broken window flowered in frost,
I talked to the snow everyday.
Summer, like all the neighbors,
refused to visit the insane.

All the prayers I'd learned in Catholic school
couldn't make her go away.

Laughter stung like a slap to my face
and I wondered how long she'd ride.

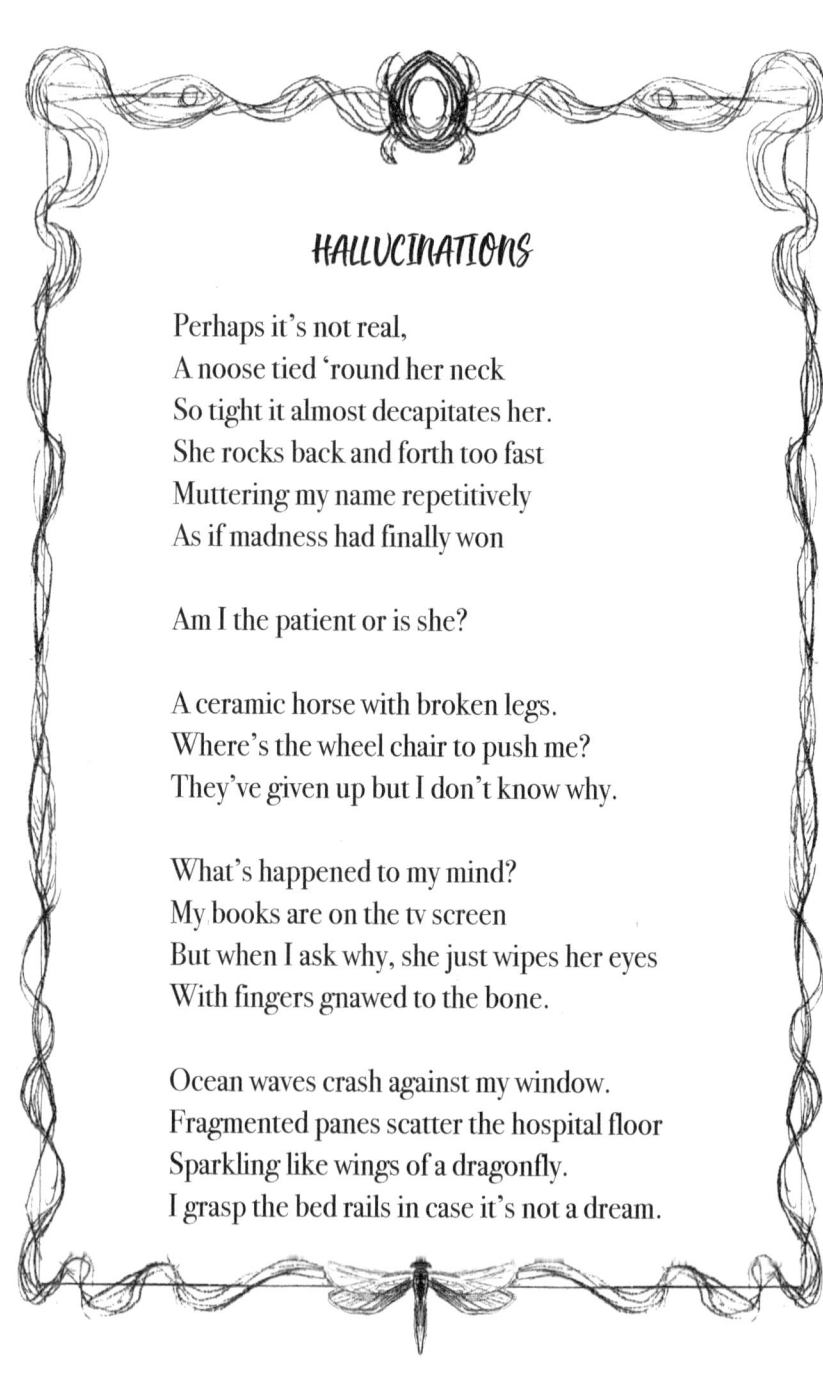

HALLUCINATIONS

Perhaps it's not real,
A noose tied 'round her neck
So tight it almost decapitates her.
She rocks back and forth too fast
Muttering my name repetitively
As if madness had finally won

Am I the patient or is she?

A ceramic horse with broken legs.
Where's the wheel chair to push me?
They've given up but I don't know why.

What's happened to my mind?
My books are on the tv screen
But when I ask why, she just wipes her eyes
With fingers gnawed to the bone.

Ocean waves crash against my window.
Fragmented panes scatter the hospital floor
Sparkling like wings of a dragonfly.
I grasp the bed rails in case it's not a dream.

Now the sea turns to mountains
I lie broken beneath miles of snow
With the taste of loathsome chemo
Frozen and bitter on my tongue.
She's calling out to me.

I am a hostage and so is she.

SOMEDAY (LIES, LIES)

How many times a day do you need to staple
Those seraphim wings to your shoulder blades?
They've grown as dirty and ragged as your promises
    and lies.
Yet no one seems to notice,
You've fooled them into benevolence your whole life.
Saint Sabastian was less a martyr than you.

Once I ripped the shedding skin from your face.
The gods cut my ring finger off with a dull blade,
Punishment for defacing a fraud.

But they'll never let me die.
I live with the lies, lies.

With you scalpel sharp tongue
In a made-up theater of grief
You fed fools stories of my woe.
Job well done, dear.
They sent money and prayers.

Three months late, the bitch
With her black umbrella
Mailed a condolence card to the dead.

STRINGS OF A CELLO

I notice her every night,
A fat girl crying
At her lover's grave
With a beat up brown case at her side.
Flowers that should have died
Ages ago still
Subsisting on her tears.
She is his obituary,
Eulogizing his life story
Under her breath.
When she thinks she's unobserved
I watch her dig handfuls of his soil
And swallow it like a penance.
She has no illusions left,
Only fools romanticize death.
I never see her arrive.
I never see her go.
But she has a mission.
Just one night in July
She removes her cello
And with all the dreams of resentment,
She plays hymns
To an audience of tombs.

THE DAY HE BECAME A STATISTIC

He's drifting away but not quickly enough
for his hospital stay.
They can barely hear a pulse.
Each time they check, nurses glare at me
as if I were to blame.

"Look closely, he's not in pain."

But I can feel a deeper ache.
He's lost the war and he knows it.
I stand alone in a bloody field,
too frightened to lay down arms.

"Medic! We need more drugs."

I am a shell-shocked soldier
lost in the dark of no-man's land.
The sound of reverential bombers overhead.

I run to a trench to catch my breath.
The hall is long and empty.
But voices keep whispering in my ear,
"Go back and say goodbye."

Kneeling down in two years of mud.
The only lie I've ever given him,
I tell him the enemy is dead.

OCTOBER

Walking in sunlight until the sky soured.
Thunder crackled, frightening the dogs.
Lightning struck a blinding blow
Fire writhed like a snake to your mind.
Our days of mercy were gone.

Trees turned black,
Three branches died in seconds.
Rain drenched our clothes
And I knew you couldn't see.

I ran and fell.
Scratched my knees
But like childhood
No one was there to comfort me.

Mystified by the future
That ran like a horror film
In murky puddles,
I watched the world drain of color.
Glanced behind me
And you were gone.

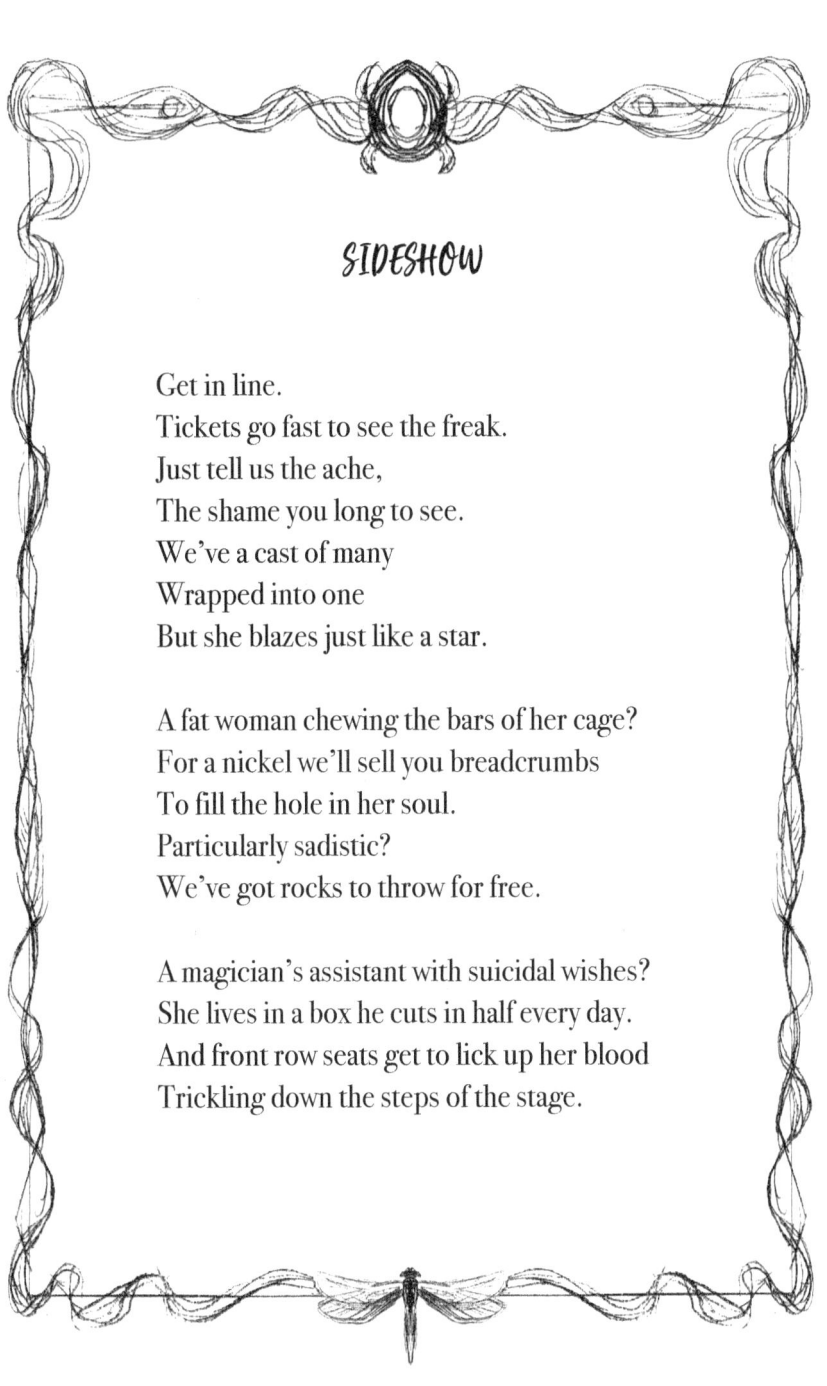

SIDESHOW

Get in line.
Tickets go fast to see the freak.
Just tell us the ache,
The shame you long to see.
We've a cast of many
Wrapped into one
But she blazes just like a star.

A fat woman chewing the bars of her cage?
For a nickel we'll sell you breadcrumbs
To fill the hole in her soul.
Particularly sadistic?
We've got rocks to throw for free.

A magician's assistant with suicidal wishes?
She lives in a box he cuts in half every day.
And front row seats get to lick up her blood
Trickling down the steps of the stage.

A pain freak without mercy?
Her arms are like an ashtray,
Grinding lit cigarettes with glee.
Want to catch an uglier scent?
Closing time she turns to melancholy.
Burns his name into her thighs
With a cigar.

THE DEPARTED COME AND GO

With a mourning song I beckoned her.
Hammered the church doors of grief
after the necromancers had hid
like lepers in a sewage ditch
forsaking the screams
of a woman dressed in the rags of madness.
.
But the witch of Endor, like a spider crab,
came crawling from the sands to me

Her velvet gown was faded red,
A castoff worn by a queen.
Shells and charms of gold and emerald
Clung to her braids like seaweed.

Her feet glided the lighthouse steps,
chanting archaic words below her breath.
I pointed to a white tipped wave
where I'd cast his ashes in a box.

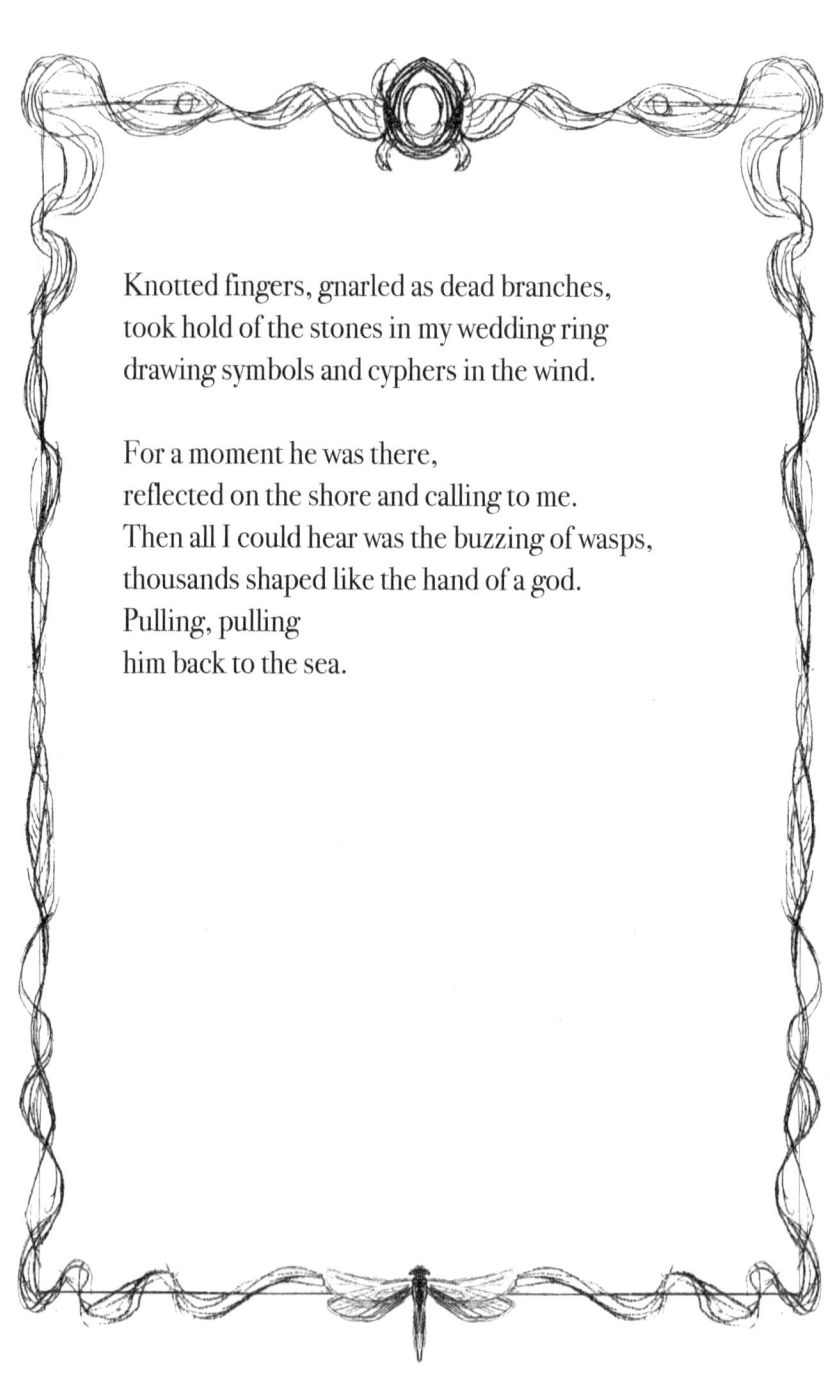

Knotted fingers, gnarled as dead branches,
took hold of the stones in my wedding ring
drawing symbols and cyphers in the wind.

For a moment he was there,
reflected on the shore and calling to me.
Then all I could hear was the buzzing of wasps,
thousands shaped like the hand of a god.
Pulling, pulling
him back to the sea.

MISTY WAS AN UGLY DOLL

When she grew weary
stubbing out cigarettes
on the old lady,
who paid dearly for
adopting a sewer rat,
Mama would come for me.

She'd lift me onto the stepping stool.
It didn't help to beg and weep,
humiliation was a sound for the weak.

With giant antique shears,
She'd chop off my hair muttering,
"Pretty girls are blonde like me."

Upstairs in the shadows,
a box with my favorite doll
"Beautiful Misty" it read in bold print.
But they were wrong,
her hair was red
and grew long with the turn of knob.

Misty cried when I cut her locks.
I had no mercy for a toy that lied.

Sometimes Mama slapped too hard
but I couldn't make Misty bleed.
So I colored bruises on her cheeks.
Now she's dead inside like me.

THE LAST WORDS OF A LOVELY LADY

She is as smartly attired
As a mannequin
In an exclusive store window
And the pearls are real.
Superiority gilded in charity,
She claims to understand my pain.

Not every widow is respectable enough
To get their 25 pence a week.
She hands me a pamphlet,
DOMESTIC RULES OF CONDUCT,
Wipes away invisible dirt
And takes her seat like a queen.

Black tape criss-crosses dirty windows
But she spies the thick dust anyway,
Runs her dove white gloves along a table.
Scrunches her pretty face as if
She smells the grief that clings to my clothes
And lingers on my skin like cologne.

I choke on the pretension in her voice.
I am beneath her. She will surely
Discuss me later at tea.

"My goodness, the run in her stockings?
And shoes so scuffed and worn.
I know she's a widow
But how difficult is it to smile."

A mistake.
She's been speaking
Of my housekeeping and strange behavior
The committee must take this all into account.
And I've been staring at his desk.

I try to grin politely
But those muscles atrophied months ago.
She snaps back as if I spit in her hair
So blonde and glorious.
I can't recall when I last brushed mine.

I walk to our wedding photograph and stare.
She talks on.
"A little rouge would put color in those cheeks"
I rummage around his papers searching.
"Neighbors say you've stopped cleaning your walk."

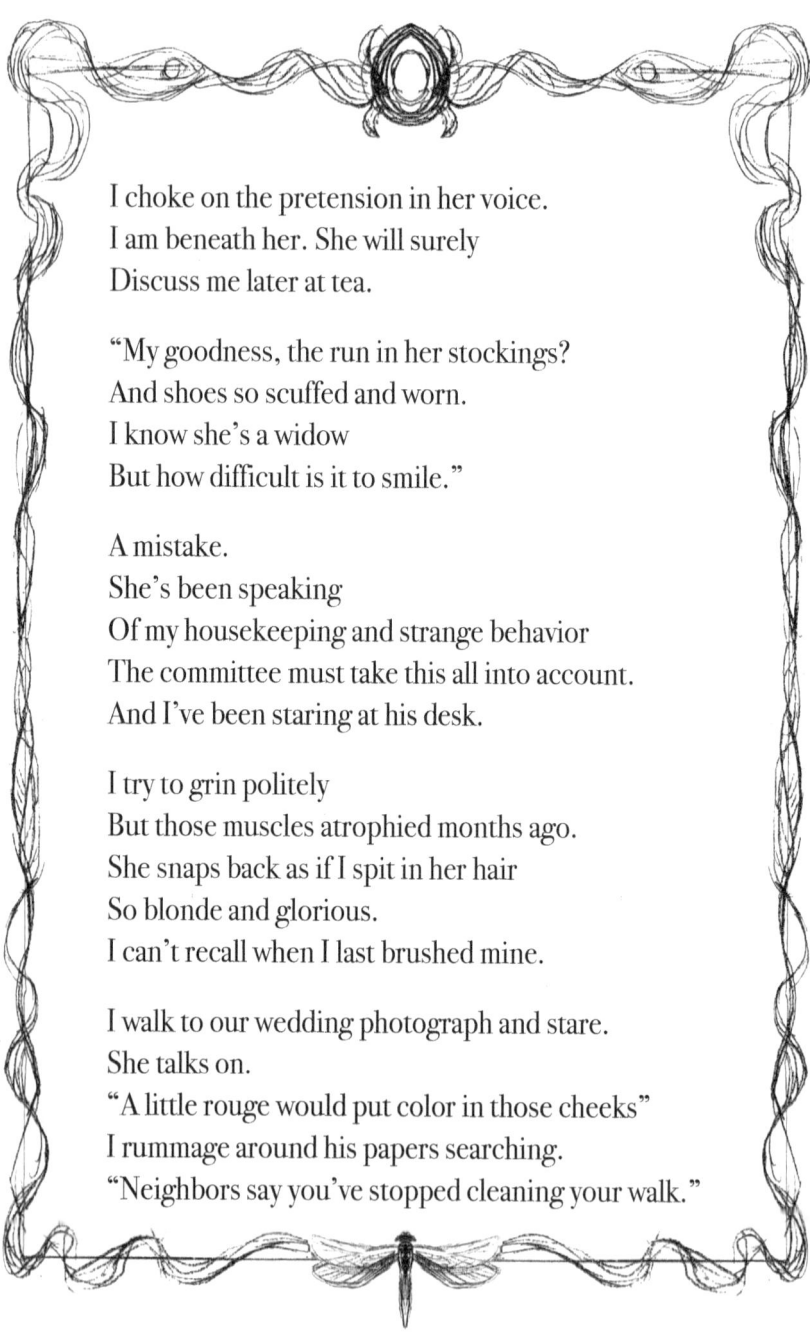

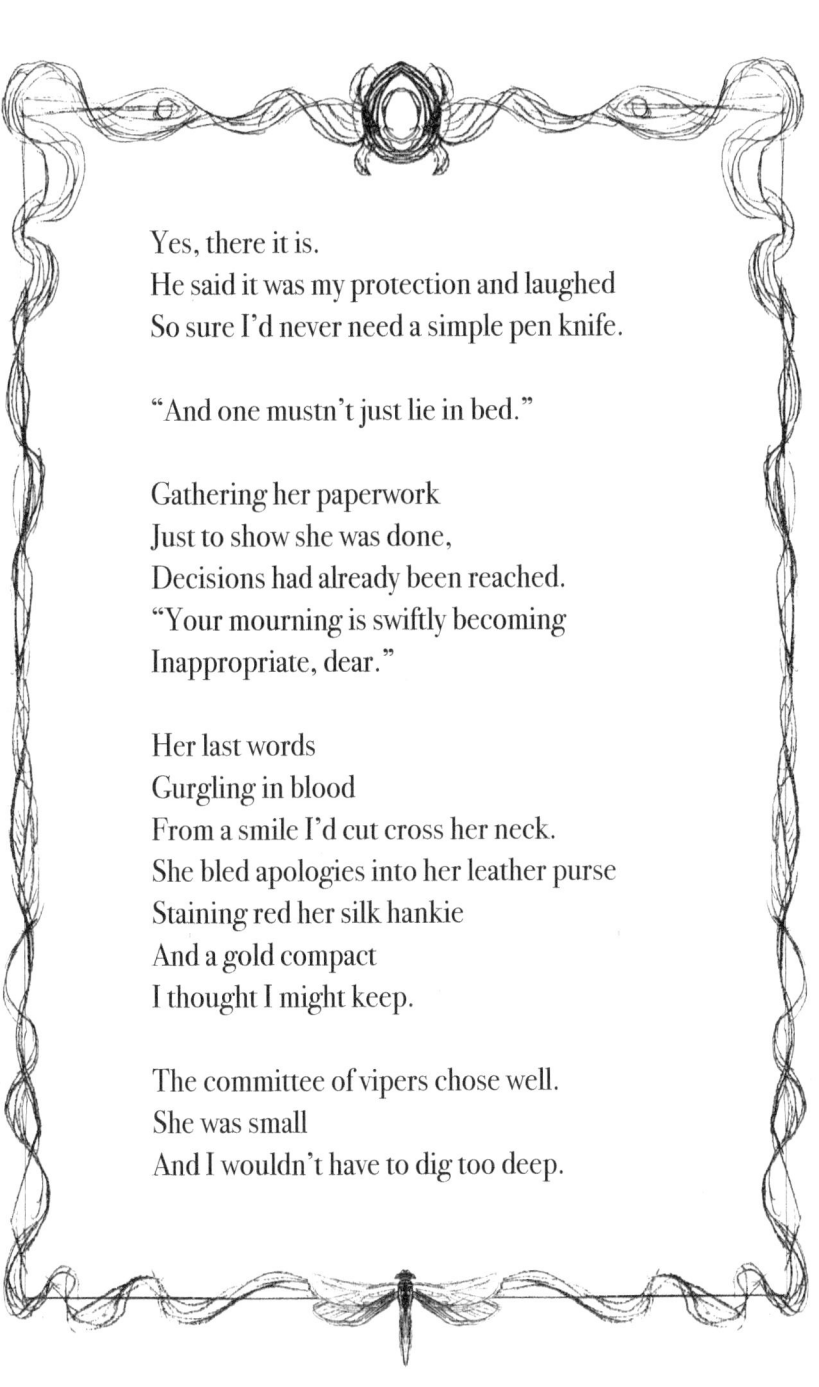

Yes, there it is.
He said it was my protection and laughed
So sure I'd never need a simple pen knife.

"And one mustn't just lie in bed."

Gathering her paperwork
Just to show she was done,
Decisions had already been reached.
"Your mourning is swiftly becoming
Inappropriate, dear."

Her last words
Gurgling in blood
From a smile I'd cut cross her neck.
She bled apologies into her leather purse
Staining red her silk hankie
And a gold compact
I thought I might keep.

The committee of vipers chose well.
She was small
And I wouldn't have to dig too deep.

THUNDER AND RAIN

There was a thunderclap
And the skies turned white.
We were never safe from the storm.
I was a fool for believing
there was ever a prize
for surviving a childhood in shackles.

You laughed when I counted
the distance after thunder roared.
A storm five miles away.

Always covering me like an umbrella.
You never told me when it struck,
just grew as silent as the walls.

Day after day the thunderstorm screamed
(I would have too if I'd known what was to come).
I watched you dreaming words
without realizing
the magic in your fingertips had died,
poems filled the gutters
and you'd slipped away in the rain.

DISQUIETING

I watch her, knowing
Someday she'll kill someone
For my pain.
It's in her eyes,
Violence searching
For an enemy to blame,
Besides a church that gave guilt
In lieu of comfort.

She screams at the nurses
When my drugs arrive late
Or the sheets aren't changed on time.
And glares at the night guards
That foolishly enter my room
Without giving a synthetic smile.

She'll never forgive anyone again.
But I'm hurling away and can't stop her.

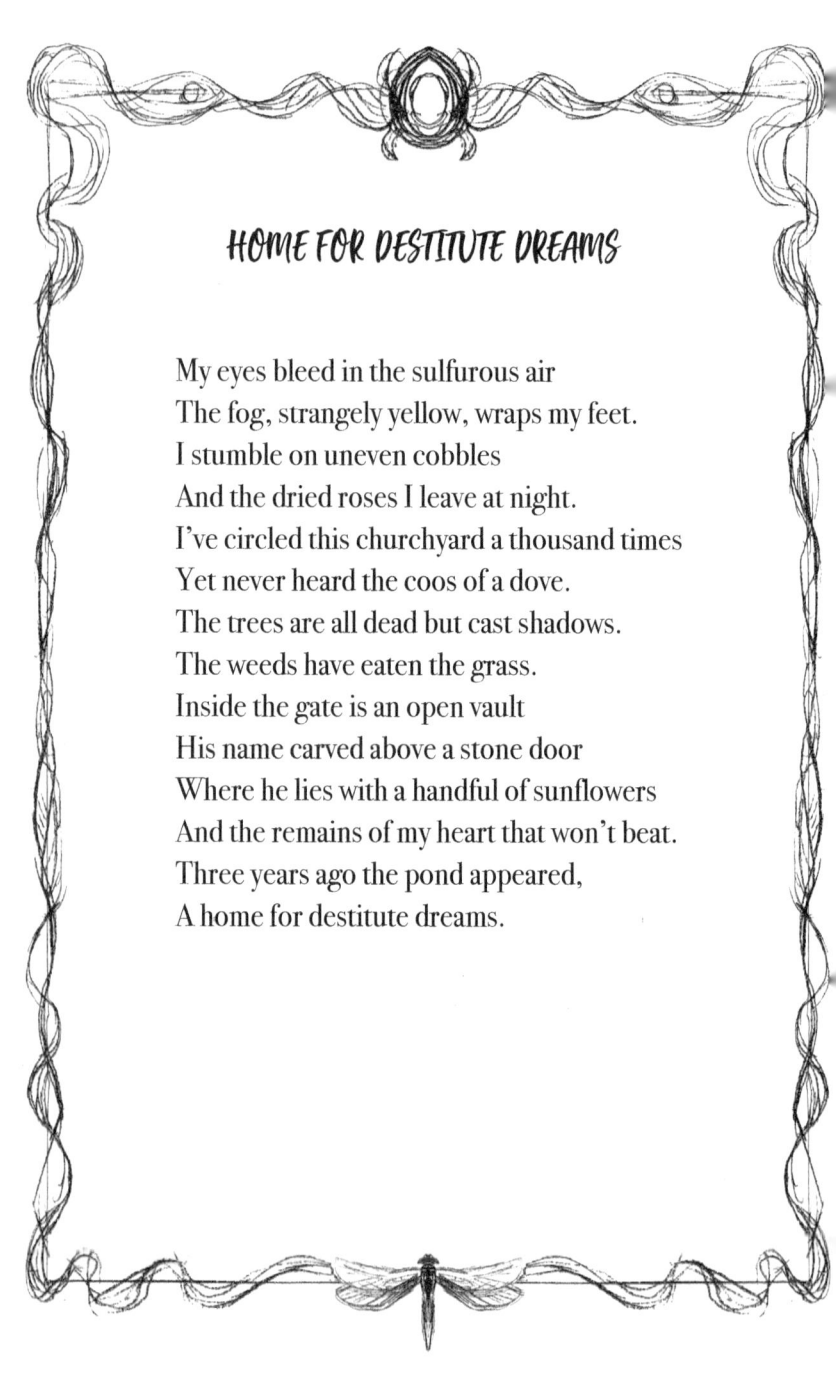

HOME FOR DESTITUTE DREAMS

My eyes bleed in the sulfurous air
The fog, strangely yellow, wraps my feet.
I stumble on uneven cobbles
And the dried roses I leave at night.
I've circled this churchyard a thousand times
Yet never heard the coos of a dove.
The trees are all dead but cast shadows.
The weeds have eaten the grass.
Inside the gate is an open vault
His name carved above a stone door
Where he lies with a handful of sunflowers
And the remains of my heart that won't beat.
Three years ago the pond appeared,
A home for destitute dreams.

EYES OF COPPER PENNIES

I want to kiss his eyes awake.
They're ready to close them
With pennies run over by a train
Before I can be sure
That he's really gone in peace
The sweet descriptive way they vowed
Repetitively, as if tedious voices
Would lull me into a stupor
And I'd let go.

Softly under my breath I growl.
"That's a new one" a nurse whispers,
Trying to joke with the others
But smart enough not to step too close.

You won't take him yet.

The wheelchair is heavy
But I pushed him for months
While they filled his mind with lies
And radiation pinpricks
Knowing all along
You can't kill giants
With a rock.

OUR SLOW DESTRUCTION

The attrition of your life
In exchange for insignificant
Sins to a god that craved
Territorial gains of your mind.
Inexplicable warfare
I knew we'd never conquer
Slowly eroded the earth
Beneath our feet.
Struggling for a shell hole
To hide away till the sun returned.
Our only defense
Toy guns filled with chemo
Artillery shells of deceit.
Now my landscape is forever altered
And you, memorialized
With dead flowers
And the poems you left behind.

WORTHY CAUSES GET TEDIOUS

In the only room saved from the bombs
With one buzzing, yellow light
They sit at a long table
Cigarette smoke and tapping pencils
Federal cogs, priests and doctors,
Social reformers with slogans
That mean nothing but rhyme nicely,
Bored women from charities
Who demand an end to donations.
"She won't get out of bed
And her walls are covered in webs."
How long is it appropriate
For her to grieve?
It's grown impossible to watch.
She wants to jump
We push her down again.
The neighbors complain
She sits outside in her bedclothes
Screaming his name
And waking their children
Who already think she's a wraith.
Has the asylum any room?

The state run home
Would do her fine.
It's not as if she'd notice
She's practically a ghost herself.

GOODBYE BLUE AUTUMN

3% chance, they said
And sent him home to wait.
Perhaps they thought the black rain
From atomic bombs going off in his brain
Were enough to keep him alive.

When he survived the first battle
(Not the war. No one wins the war)
He crawled to his desk. His home.
And pulled out the fragments of a story
That slipped from his hands when a blast
Pushed him down the stairs,
And stole the color from his eyes.

Wandering in foggy imaginings
For a time
He was no longer the shell of disease.

He stood on railroad tracks with a little dog
Waiting in the nights of Blue Autumn
For the train he had named Nightingale.

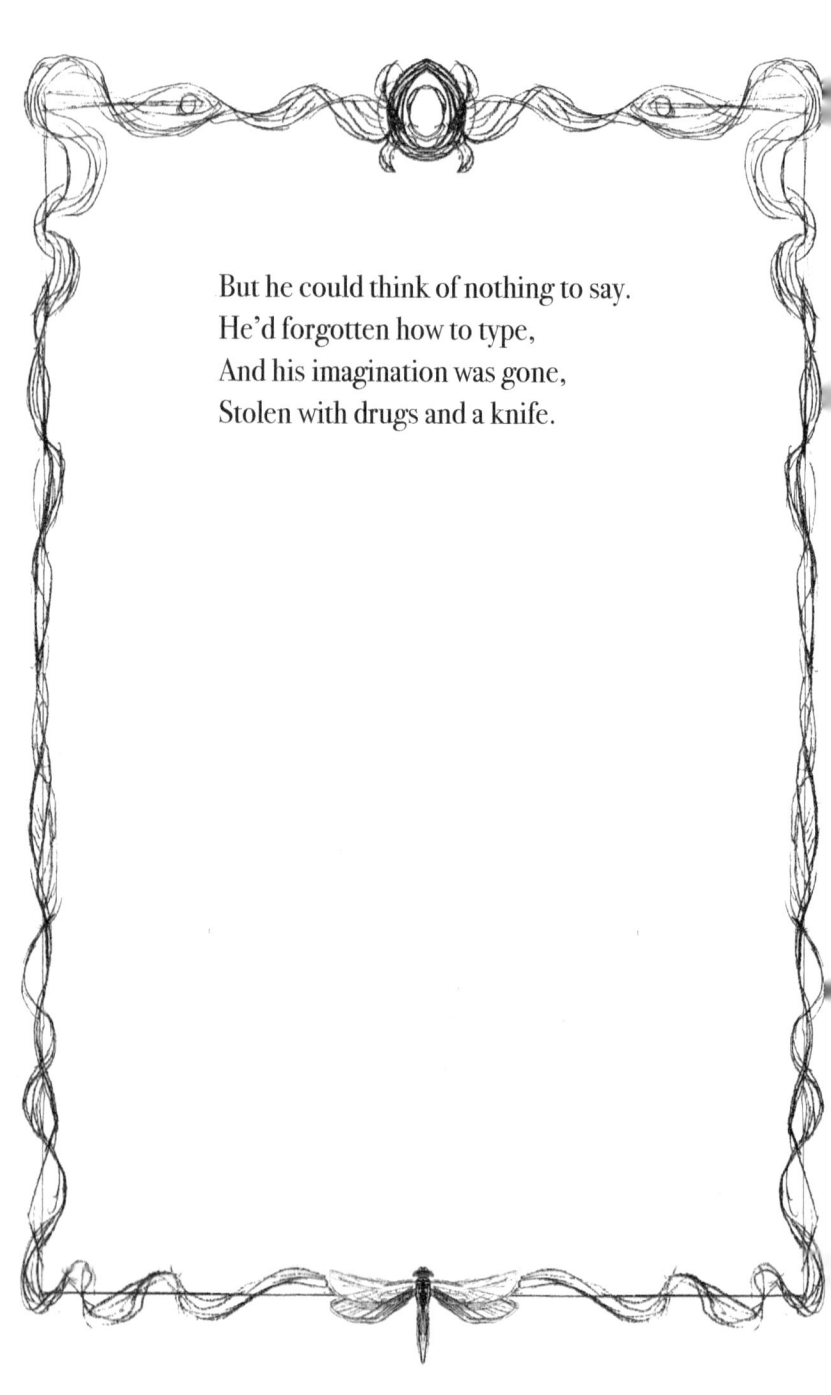

But he could think of nothing to say.
He'd forgotten how to type,
And his imagination was gone,
Stolen with drugs and a knife.

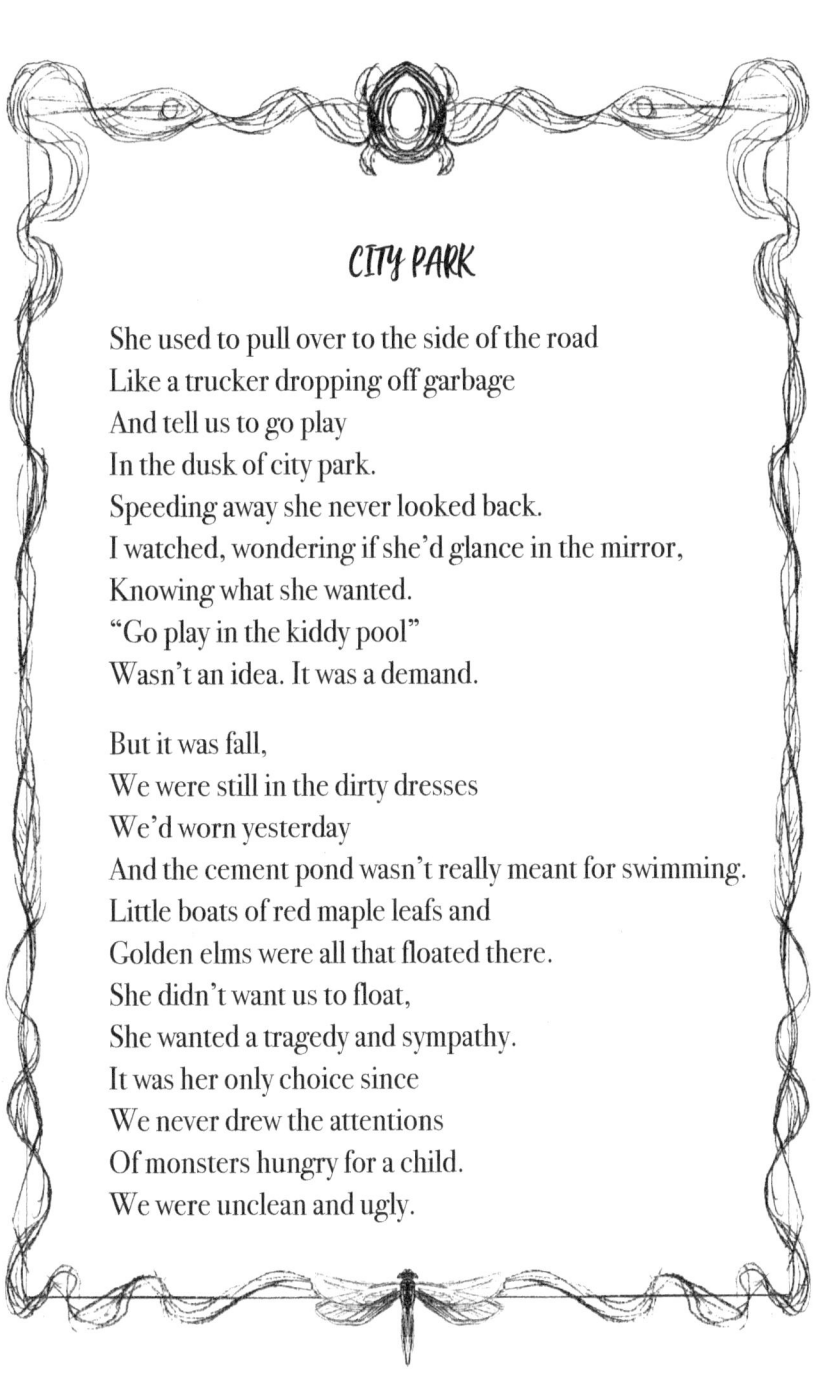

CITY PARK

She used to pull over to the side of the road
Like a trucker dropping off garbage
And tell us to go play
In the dusk of city park.
Speeding away she never looked back.
I watched, wondering if she'd glance in the mirror,
Knowing what she wanted.
"Go play in the kiddy pool"
Wasn't an idea. It was a demand.

But it was fall,
We were still in the dirty dresses
We'd worn yesterday
And the cement pond wasn't really meant for swimming.
Little boats of red maple leafs and
Golden elms were all that floated there.
She didn't want us to float,
She wanted a tragedy and sympathy.
It was her only choice since
We never drew the attentions
Of monsters hungry for a child.
We were unclean and ugly.

But there was always the pool.
She dreamed of our heads cracked like Easter eggs.
Blood replacing the water
If we'd just tilt back on the stone edge
When we played.

A boy from our school watched
From the safety of his window
Across the street
And wondered if the shadow of tree branches
Would gather us up one night.

LOT'S WIFE

They forced her into the future
letting it tear her to shreds
before she could blink away
what was to come.
What she wouldn't forget
if they stoned her to death.
A world without light
to keep the demons at bay,
more evil than anything
she'd screamed about in nightmares.
"Look ahead," she was warned by
faces blank as sheets of parchment.
A belt around her neck
pulling her into fate.
Her eyes sewn open,
Dry as the desert.
"This is your tomorrow,"
But the truth was louder than their god.
There was no sun before her,
just shadows so gray
a beam of light couldn't labor through.

Sand turning to snow,
wind kissing her lips until they bled.
Fingers turned to brittle bones
Until her ring slid off with her skin.
"Hurry!" they cried
dragging her closer to a room
without doors,
without hope.
Breaking free she knelt to the image of yesterday,
drowning in her own sea of salt and tears.

ABOUT THE AUTHOR

Since 1994 Michelle Scalise's work has appeared in such anthologies as Unspeakable Horror, Darker Side, Dark Arts, The Big Book of Erotic Ghost Stories, Best Women's Erotica, Dark Voices and such magazines as Cemetery Dance, Space And Time, Crimewave and Dark Discoveries. She was nominated for the 2010 Spectrum Award which honors outstanding works of fantasy and horror that include positive gay characters. Her poetry has been nominated for the Elgin Award and the Rhysling Award. Her fiction has received honorable mention in Years Best Fantasy and Horror. Her poems have appeared in the Horror Writers Association anthology Horror Poetry Showcase: Vol I and II. SFSite chose her first collection, Intervals of Horrible Sanity, as one of the top ten books of 2003. Her fiction/poetry collection , Collective Suicide, was published by Crossroad Press in 2012. In 2014 Eldritch Press published a collection of her poetry, The Manufacture of Sorrow in paperback. It became a bestseller in the women writer's category on Amazon and was nominated for the Elgin Award. Michelle is the wife of bestselling author Tom Piccirilli.

www.ingramcontent.com/pod-product-compliance
Lightning Source LLC
Chambersburg PA
CBHW060507080526
44584CB00015B/1580